I0104740

Kilmann-Saxton
Culture-Gap®
Survey

RALPH H. KILMANN

MARY J. SAXTON

Copyright © 1991 to 2011 by Organizational Design Consultants (ODC). All rights reserved. This material may not be reproduced, stored in a retrieval system, or transmitted in any form by any means—electronic, mechanical, photocopying, video recording, or otherwise—without the prior written permission from ODC. Contact: ralph@kilmann.com.

Culture-Gap is a registered trademark of
Organizational Design Consultants

Distributed by
KILMANN DIAGNOSTICS
1 Suprema Drive
Newport Coast, CA 92657
www.kilmanndiagnostics.com
info@kilmanndiagnostics.com
949.497.8766

Introducing Culture-Gaps

The culture of a work group is the invisible force that guides behavior. It is not what the formal policies, rules, procedures, and job descriptions mandate. Rather, culture is the unwritten—often unconscious—message that fills in the gaps between what is formally decreed and what actually takes place. Culture, therefore, determines how formal statements get interpreted and provides what the written documents leave out. As a result, culture affects the quality of decision making and action taking, which in turn affects work group morale and performance.

While culture manifests itself in several ways, it is most subject to measurement and change through work group norms. These norms are the unwritten "rules of the game," what really counts in order to get ahead or, alternatively, how to stay out of trouble. The Kilmann-Saxton Culture-Gap Survey provides a systematic tool for pinpointing cultural norms. Part 1 of this survey assesses the actual norms that are operating in your work group. Part 2 assesses the desired norms that would improve your group's performance, job satisfaction, and morale. Differences between actual and desired norms are referred to as "Culture-Gaps."

Once you have completed Parts 1 and 2 of this survey, you will be able to graph your own Culture-Gap Profile. If you have access to the other members in your work group, department, or the entire organization, you can graph additional Culture-Gap Profiles. These various profiles will enable you to pinpoint the particular Culture-Gaps that are barriers to organizational success.

COPYRIGHT © 1991–2011 BY ORGANIZATIONAL DESIGN CONSULTANTS. ALL RIGHTS RESERVED.

Part 1: Actual Norms

What really goes on in your organization? What does it take to get ahead? How do you stay out of trouble? What does your boss really want from you?

To answer these questions, every work group develops its own "rules of the game" and then pressures each member to follow them. While these norms, as they are called, are seldom written down or discussed, this survey enables you to identify the ones that are operating in your group. You may not agree with the usefulness of these norms nor do you always follow them. But they do influence what goes on in your work group.

On the following pages are 28 pairs of norms. For each pair, please circle the "A" or "B" which best describes the *actual* norm in your group. If you are a member of more than one group, complete the survey for the group where you spend most of your time and effort. In some cases both the "A" and "B" norms may be operating, but please circle the one that is operating most strongly most of the time.

Note: It is important that you choose the "A" or "B" norm according to *the pressures your work group puts on its members*. This may be quite different from how you do behave, or how you would like to behave, in your work group.

COPYRIGHT © 1991–2011 BY ORGANIZATIONAL DESIGN CONSULTANTS. ALL RIGHTS RESERVED.

1. A.   Put down the work of other groups.

    B.   Support the work of other groups.

2. A.   Encourage creativity.

    B.   Discourage creativity.

3. A.   Don't socialize with your work group.

    B.   Socialize with your work group.

4. A.   Dress as you like.

    B.   Dress in the accepted manner.

5. A.   Share information to help other groups.

    B.   Share information with other groups only when it benefits your own work group.

6. A.   Keep things the same.

    B.   Make changes.

7. A.   Mixing friendships with business is fine.

    B.   Don't mix friendships with business.

8. A.   Don't go outside the regular lines of communication.

    B.   Feel free to communicate with anyone.

COPYRIGHT © 1991–2011 BY ORGANIZATIONAL DESIGN CONSULTANTS. ALL RIGHTS RESERVED.

9. A. Don't divide and assign work fairly.

     B. Divide and assign work fairly.

10. A. Try new ways of doing things.

     B. Don't "rock the boat."

11. A. Don't develop friendships with your co-workers.

     B. Develop friendships with your co-workers.

12. A. Use your own judgement in following rules and regulations.

     B. Comply with all rules and regulations.

13. A. Complete all tasks in the best possible way.

     B. Do as little as necessary to get by.

14. A. Don't try to change.

     B. Always try to improve.

15. A. Encourage socializing on the job.

     B. Discourage socializing on the job.

16. A. Please the organization.

     B. Do what pleases you.

COPYRIGHT © 1991–2011 BY ORGANIZATIONAL DESIGN CONSULTANTS. ALL RIGHTS RESERVED.

17. A. Share information only when it benefits you.

    B. Share information to help the organization make better decisions.

18. A. Help others put new ideas into practice.

    B. Resist putting new ideas into practice.

19. A. Don't bother getting to know the people in your work group.

    B. Get to know the people in your work group.

20. A. Express your personal preferences on the job.

    B. Keep your personal preferences to yourself.

21. A. Help others complete their tasks.

    B. Concentrate only on your own tasks.

22. A. Resist taking on new tasks.

    B. Be willing to take on new tasks.

23. A. Participate in social activities with others in your organization.

    B. Don't participate in social activities with others in your organization.

COPYRIGHT © 1991–2011 BY ORGANIZATIONAL DESIGN CONSULTANTS. ALL RIGHTS RESERVED.

24. A. Live for your job or career.

    B. Live for yourself or your family.

25. A. Compete with other work groups.

    B. Cooperate with other work groups.

26. A. Encourage new ideas.

    B. Discourage new ideas.

27. A. Don't socialize with those in other work groups.

    B. Socialize with those in other work groups.

28. A. Believe in your own values.

    B. Believe in the organization's values.

COPYRIGHT © 1991–2011 BY ORGANIZATIONAL DESIGN CONSULTANTS. ALL RIGHTS RESERVED.

Part 2: Desired Norms

You just circled the actual norms that are operating in your work group. Now you are asked to choose which of these norms **should be** operating in order to increase performance, job satisfaction, and morale.

On the following pages are the same 28 pairs of norms. For each pair, please circle the "A" or "B" which best represents the **desired** norm for your work group.

COPYRIGHT © 1991–2011 BY ORGANIZATIONAL DESIGN CONSULTANTS. ALL RIGHTS RESERVED.

29. A. Put down the work of other groups.

    B. Support the work of other groups.

30. A. Encourage creativity.

    B. Discourage creativity.

31. A. Don't socialize with your work group.

    B. Socialize with your work group.

32. A. Dress as you like.

    B. Dress in the accepted manner.

33. A. Share information to help other groups.

    B. Share information with other groups only when it benefits your own work group.

34. A. Keep things the same.

    B. Make changes.

35. A. Mixing friendships with business is fine.

    B. Don't mix friendships with business.

36. A. Don't go outside the regular lines of communication.

    B. Feel free to communicate with anyone.

COPYRIGHT © 1991–2011 BY ORGANIZATIONAL DESIGN CONSULTANTS. ALL RIGHTS RESERVED.

37. A. Don't divide and assign work fairly.

    B. Divide and assign work fairly.

38. A. Try new ways of doing things.

    B. Don't "rock the boat."

39. A. Don't develop friendships with your co-workers.

    B. Develop friendships with your co-workers.

40. A. Use your own judgement in following rules and regulations.

    B. Comply with all rules and regulations.

41. A. Complete all tasks in the best possible way.

    B. Do as little as necessary to get by.

42. A. Don't try to change.

    B. Always try to improve.

43. A. Encourage socializing on the job.

    B. Discourage socializing on the job.

44. A. Please the organization.

    B. Do what pleases you.

COPYRIGHT © 1991–2011 BY ORGANIZATIONAL DESIGN CONSULTANTS. ALL RIGHTS RESERVED.

45. A. Share information only when it benefits you.

    B. Share information to help the organization make better decisions.

46. A. Help others put new ideas into practice.

    B. Resist putting new ideas into practice.

47. A. Don't bother getting to know the people in your work group.

    B. Get to know the people in your work group.

48. A. Express your personal preferences on the job.

    B. Keep your personal preferences to yourself.

49. A. Help others complete their tasks.

    B. Concentrate only on your own tasks.

50. A. Resist taking on new tasks.

    B. Be willing to take on new tasks.

51. A. Participate in social activities with others in your organization.

    B. Don't participate in social activities with others in your organization.

COPYRIGHT © 1991–2011 BY ORGANIZATIONAL DESIGN CONSULTANTS. ALL RIGHTS RESERVED.

52. A. Live for your job or career.

    B. Live for yourself or your family.

53. A. Compete with other work groups.

    B. Cooperate with other work groups.

54. A. Encourage new ideas.

    B. Discourage new ideas.

55. A. Don't socialize with those in other work groups.

    B. Socialize with those in other work groups.

56. A. Believe in your own values.

    B. Believe in the organization's values.

COPYRIGHT © 1991–2011 BY ORGANIZATIONAL DESIGN CONSULTANTS. ALL RIGHTS RESERVED.

Scoring Your Responses

On the opposite page is your scoring sheet. Please circle the letters that you circled on the survey. It is easiest to score Part 1 first (from item 1 to 28) and Part 2 next (from item 29 to 56). If any "A" or "B" norm that you circled on the survey is not listed on the scoring sheet, simply skip the item and go on to the next one.

For each column, sum the number of letters you circled. Then subtract all the sums as shown. The resulting four calculations in the shaded areas are your four Culture-Gap scores: Task Support, Task Innovation, Social Relationships, and Personal Freedom. Be sure to show a minus sign (–) on any Culture-Gap score if the sum on the right column is larger than the sum on the left column (for example: $4 - 6 = -2$). Otherwise show a plus sign (for example: $6 - 4 = +2$).

COPYRIGHT © 1991–2011 BY ORGANIZATIONAL DESIGN CONSULTANTS. ALL RIGHTS RESERVED.

CULTURE-GAP® SURVEY

PART 2	PART 1		PART 2	PART 1
29. B	1. B		30. A	2. A
33. A	5. A		34. B	6. B
37. B	9. B		38. A	10. A
41. A	13. A		42. B	14. B
45. B	17. B		46. A	18. A
49. A	21. A		50. B	22. B
53. B	25. B		54. A	26. A

☐ − ☐ = ☐
SUM   SUM   *Task Support*

☐ − ☐ = ☐
SUM   SUM   *Task Innovation*

PART 2	PART 1		PART 2	PART 1
31. B	3. B		32. A	4. A
35. A	7. A		36. B	8. B
39. B	11. B		40. A	12. A
43. A	15. A		44. B	16. B
47. B	19. B		48. A	20. A
51. A	23. A		52. B	24. B
55. B	27. B		56. A	28. A

☐ − ☐ = ☐
SUM   SUM   *Social Relationships*

☐ − ☐ = ☐
SUM   SUM   *Personal Freedom*

COPYRIGHT © 1991–2011 BY ORGANIZATIONAL DESIGN CONSULTANTS. ALL RIGHTS RESERVED.

Graphing Your Culture-Gap® Profile

The four scores that you just calculated can be summarized as a Culture-Gap Profile. This profile shows the four scores plotted in bar-graph form for easy interpretation.

Please transfer each of your four scores from the scoring sheet to the indicated place on the opposite page. Disregarding the plus or minus sign (+ or –) of each score for now, draw a straight line to represent the height of each bar graph. For example, if your score for Task Support is +5, then draw a straight line from the left to the right hand side of the shaded bar graph, where 5 is shown. If your score for Task Innovation is –3, then draw a straight line where 3 is shown. Do this for all four scores. Should any of your scores be 0, disregard the bar graph for that score.

Now, for each score that has a plus sign (+), please fill in the shaded bar with your pen or pencil, from the line you drew down to the base of the bar. For each score that has a minus sign (–), just darken the side lines of the bar (from the line you drew down to the base), leaving the rest unfilled. Two different types of bar graphs are thereby possible:

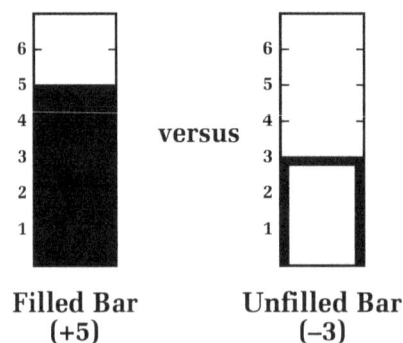

Filled Bar **versus** **Unfilled Bar**
(+5) **(–3)**

COPYRIGHT © 1991–2011 BY ORGANIZATIONAL DESIGN CONSULTANTS. ALL RIGHTS RESERVED.

Task
Support

Task
Innovation

Social
Relationships

Personal
Freedom

Culture-Gap® Profile

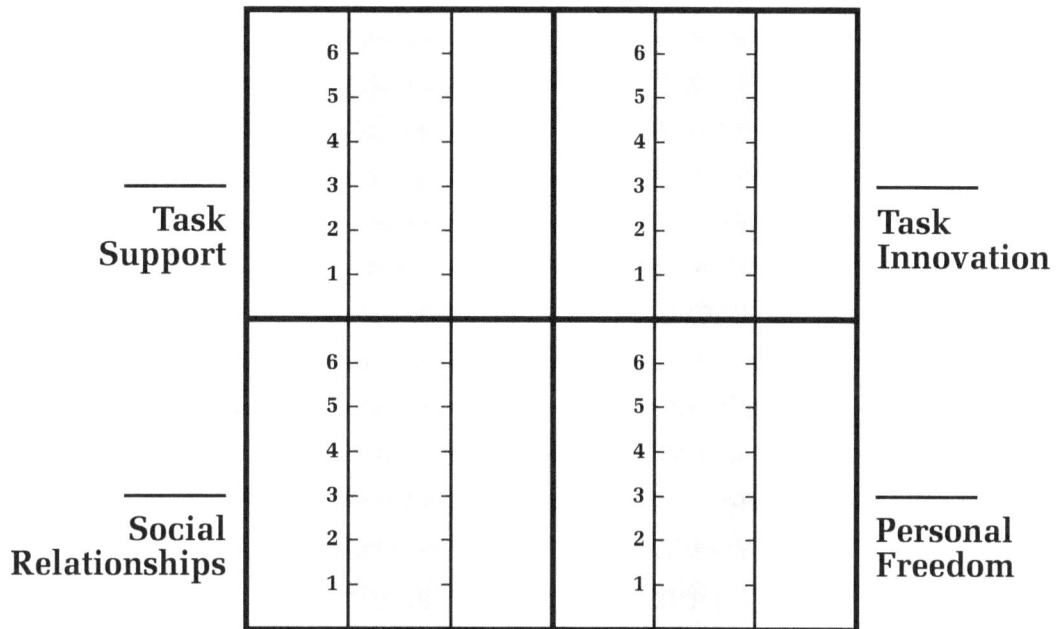

COPYRIGHT © 1991–2011 BY ORGANIZATIONAL DESIGN CONSULTANTS. ALL RIGHTS RESERVED.

Developing Organizational Profiles

Once all the individuals in your work group have obtained and graphed their scores on the four Culture-Gaps, collect all these numbers together on a separate sheet of paper and then calculate four averages: a group average for Task Support, Task Innovation, Social Relationships, and Personal Freedom. While computing these four averages, make sure to divide the sum of the scores for each Culture-Gap by the right number of individuals in your group: those who actually provided their scores for these calculations. Also, please be sure to include the right sign (+ or −) for each Culture-Gap score in all calculations.

Once the four averages have been calculated for your work group, please enter the results in the appropriate spaces on the opposite page. Then, as you did for your individual scores, use a pen or pencil to fill in the four bar graphs for **1. My Work Group**. Next, if you have access to the other work groups in your department, you can calculate and graph the four averages for **2. My Department**. And, if you have access to all the departments in your organization, you can also calculate and graph the four averages for **3. My Organization**. For your convenience, subsequent pages provide these Culture-Gap Profiles, including a space to enter the number of respondents (N) included in the analysis. Note: In calculating these various profiles, you might find it useful to weigh the averages of each particular group by the number of its members—to adjust for different sizes of groups and departments in your organization.

COPYRIGHT © 1991–2011 BY ORGANIZATIONAL DESIGN CONSULTANTS. ALL RIGHTS RESERVED.

1. My Work Group (N = _____)

```
Task                    Task
Support                 Innovation


Social                  Personal
Relationships           Freedom
```

Culture-Gap® Profile

COPYRIGHT © 1991–2011 BY ORGANIZATIONAL DESIGN CONSULTANTS. ALL RIGHTS RESERVED.

2. My Department (N = _____)

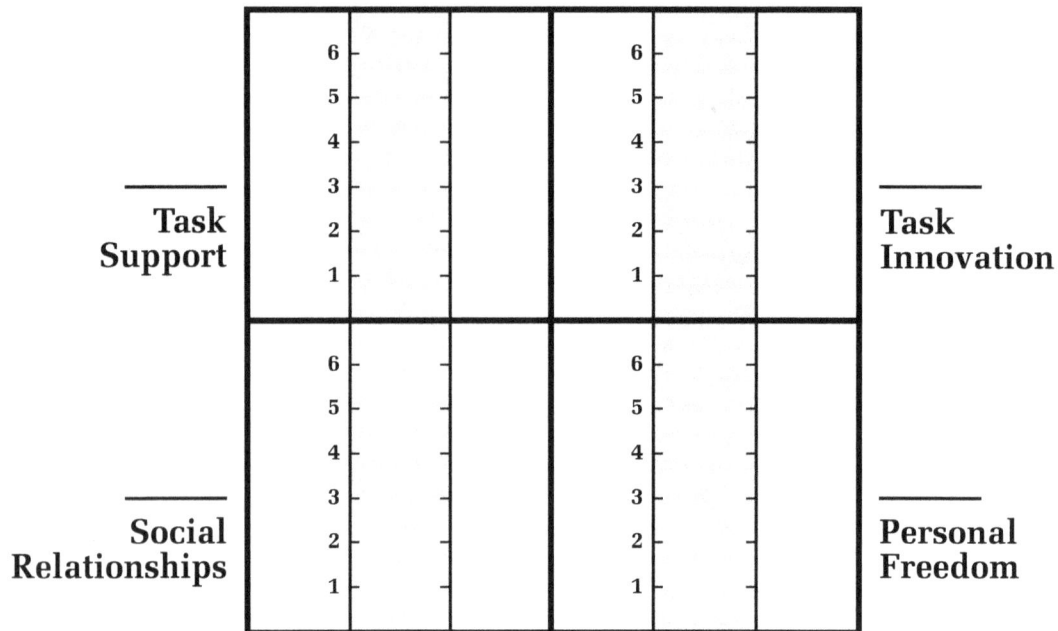

Task Support	6 5 4 3 2 1	6 5 4 3 2 1	**Task Innovation**
Social Relationships	6 5 4 3 2 1	6 5 4 3 2 1	**Personal Freedom**

Culture-Gap® Profile

COPYRIGHT © 1991–2011 BY ORGANIZATIONAL DESIGN CONSULTANTS. ALL RIGHTS RESERVED.

3. My Organization (N = _____)

	Task Support				Task Innovation
6			6		
5			5		
4			4		
3			3		
2			2		
1			1		
6			6		
5			5		
4			4		
3			3		
2			2		
1			1		

_____
Task
Support

_____
Task
Innovation

_____
Social
Relationships

_____
Personal
Freedom

Culture-Gap® Profile

COPYRIGHT © 1991–2011 BY ORGANIZATIONAL DESIGN CONSULTANTS. ALL RIGHTS RESERVED.

Defining Four Culture-Gaps

As shown on the opposite page, the four Culture-Gap scores are defined by two independent distinctions: (1) technical versus human concerns, as functioning (2) short term versus long term.

The technical/human distinction examines cultural norms that influence the technical aspects of work with norms that influence the social and personal aspects. This fundamental distinction has appeared in virtually all discussions of behavior in organizations—as task orientation versus people orientation.

The short-term/long-term distinction examines those cultural norms that function on a day-to-day basis versus norms that focus on the future of the organization. The latter type includes norms that emphasize work improvements (rather than just getting today's work done), and norms that define the relationship between individuals and their organization (rather than focusing on daily social interactions).

Since these two basic distinctions cover such a wide spectrum of life in an organization, the resulting four types of Culture-Gaps are expected to capture the variety of cultural norms that affect organizational success as well as job satisfaction.

COPYRIGHT © 1991–2011 BY ORGANIZATIONAL DESIGN CONSULTANTS. ALL RIGHTS RESERVED.

TECHNICAL
CONCERNS

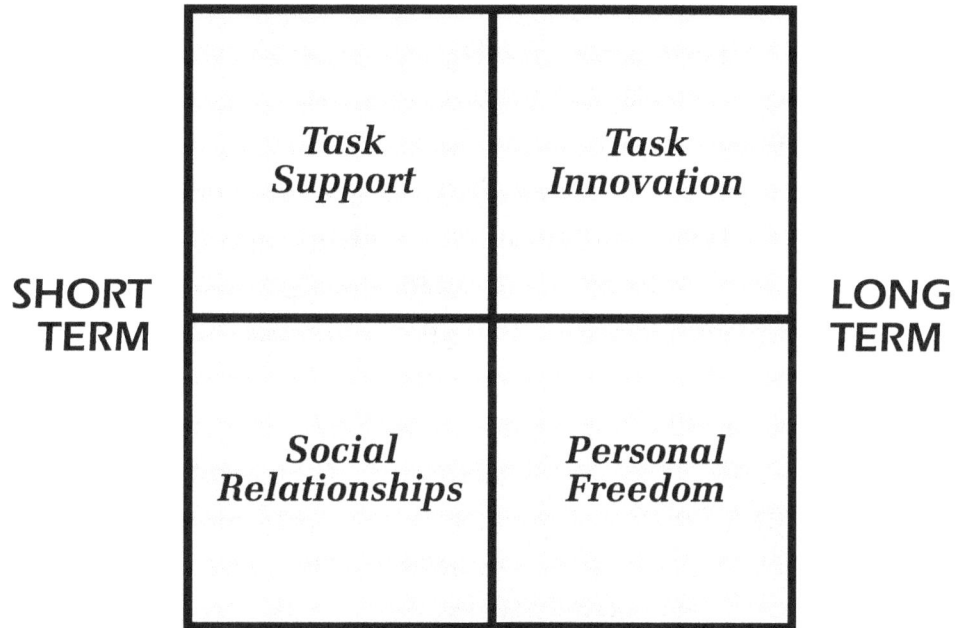

Task Support	*Task Innovation*
Social Relationships	*Personal Freedom*

SHORT TERM

LONG TERM

HUMAN
CONCERNS

COPYRIGHT © 1991–2011 BY ORGANIZATIONAL DESIGN CONSULTANTS. ALL RIGHTS RESERVED.

Task Support includes norms that are technical in nature with a short time frame. An unfilled bar in this quadrant (a Culture-Gap score with a minus sign) indicates that performance and morale would be improved by a change toward *less* Task Support. A filled bar (a Culture-Gap score with a plus sign) indicates improvement can be accomplished by a change toward *more* Task Support. For example, the first norm in each of the following norm pairs represents a change toward less Task Support while the second norm shows a change toward more Task Support: "Share information with other groups only when it benefits your own work group" versus "Share information to help other groups." "Concentrate only on your own tasks" versus "Help others complete their tasks."

Task Innovation includes norms that are technical in nature with a long time frame. An unfilled bar in this quadrant (a Culture-Gap score with a minus sign) indicates that performance and morale would be improved by a change toward *less* Task Innovation. A filled bar (a Culture-Gap score with a plus sign) indicates improvement can be accomplished by a change toward *more* Task Innovation. For example, a change toward less or more Task Innovation, respectively, is demonstrated in each of these norm pairs: "Keep things the same" versus "Make changes." "Discourage creativity" versus "Encourage creativity."

COPYRIGHT © 1991–2011 BY ORGANIZATIONAL DESIGN CONSULTANTS. ALL RIGHTS RESERVED.

Social Relationships includes norms that have a people orientation with a short time frame. An unfilled bar in this quadrant (a Culture-Gap with a minus sign) indicates that performance and morale would be improved by a change toward *less* Social Relationships. A filled bar (a Culture-Gap with a plus sign) indicates improvement can be accomplished by a change toward *more* Social Relationships. For example, a change toward less or more Social Relationships, respectively, is demonstrated in each of these norm pairs: "Don't participate in social activities with others in your organization" versus "Participate in social activities with others in your organization." "Don't bother getting to know the people in your work group" versus "Get to know the people in your work group."

Personal Freedom includes norms that have a people orientation with a long time frame. An unfilled bar in this quadrant (a Culture-Gap score with a minus sign) indicates that performance and morale would be improved by a change toward *less* Personal Freedom. A filled bar (a Culture-Gap score with a plus sign) indicates that improvement can be accomplished by a change toward *more* Personal Freedom. For example, a change toward less or more Personal Freedom, respectively, is demonstrated in each of these norm pairs: "Live for your job or career" versus "Live for yourself or your family." "Believe in the organization's values" versus "Believe in your own values."

COPYRIGHT © 1991–2011 BY ORGANIZATIONAL DESIGN CONSULTANTS. ALL RIGHTS RESERVED.

Interpreting Your Scores

Since each Culture-Gap score is derived from individual responses to seven norm pairs, each score can range from 0 to +7 or –7 (scores can be plus or minus). The following diagnostic guidelines suggest what Culture-Gap scores need special attention:

A score of +3 or higher (a filled bar) in any quadrant represents, very possibly, a significant Culture-Gap. It reveals a desire for more Task Support, more Task Innovation, more Social Relationships, or more Personal Freedom—depending on the quadrant in question. A score of +1 suggests an insignificant Culture-Gap. A score of +2 is borderline.

Any minus score (an unfilled bar) represents, potentially, a significant Culture-Gap. Such a score indicates a desire for less Task Support, less Task Innovation, less Social Relationships, or less Personal Freedom—depending on the quadrant in question. Since unfilled bars tend to occur infrequently as compared to filled bars, any unfilled bar should thus be considered as a possible cultural barrier to organizational success.

If as many as three or four scores in any Culture-Gap Profile are found to be significant according to these diagnostic guidelines, a rather broad-based cultural problem is evident. Here a variety of Culture-Gaps are collectively hindering the performance, job satisfaction, and morale of the work unit.

COPYRIGHT © 1991–2011 BY ORGANIZATIONAL DESIGN CONSULTANTS. ALL RIGHTS RESERVED.

An Example: My Work Group (N = 10)

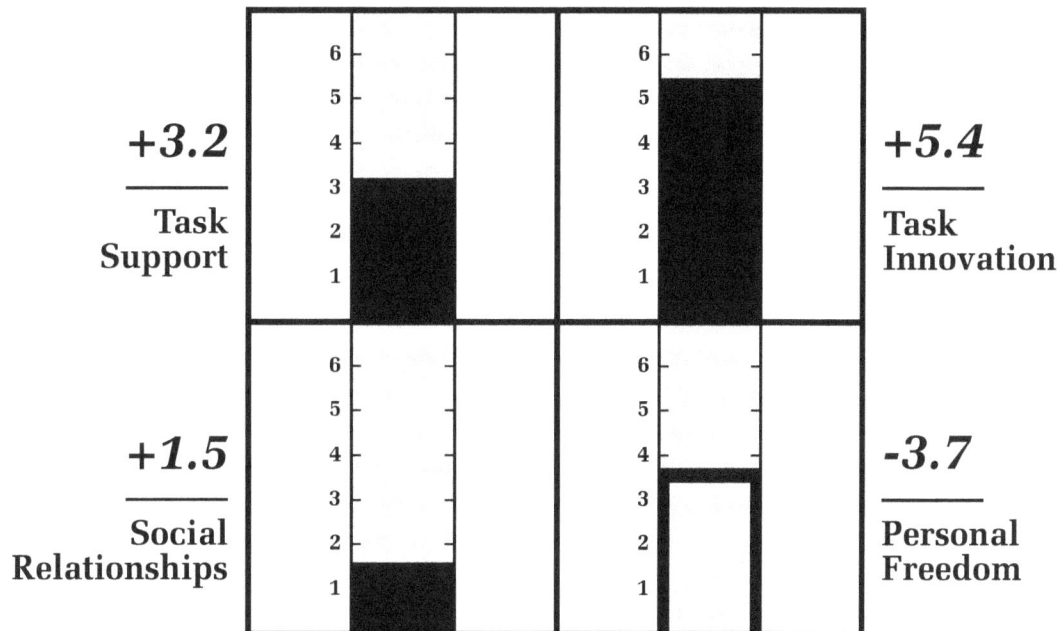

+3.2
——
Task
Support

+5.4
——
Task
Innovation

+1.5
——
Social
Relationships

-3.7
——
Personal
Freedom

Culture-Gap® Profile

COPYRIGHT © 1991–2011 BY ORGANIZATIONAL DESIGN CONSULTANTS. ALL RIGHTS RESERVED.

As revealed by the example Culture-Gap Profile on the previous page, the technical norms of this work group do not seem to encourage the necessary information sharing and support for getting the day-to-day work done (Task Support = +3.2). Even more pronounced, the actual norms do not encourage the necessary creative and innovative behavior that is required (Task Innovation = +5.4). Taken together, the technical norms are most likely interfering with performance and morale—both short term and long term.

In the same example, the norms concerned with the human aspects of organizational life uncover an insignificant Culture-Gap for day-to-day social interactions (Social Relationships = +1.5). Examining the long-term relationship between individuals and their organization, however, an unfilled bar (a minus Culture-Gap score) reveals a significant culture problem. (Personal Freedom = −3.7). The culture might encourage too much choice in following standard operating procedures, yet members realize that a closer adherence to organizational guidelines is necessary for success.

Since three of the four Culture-Gaps achieve a significant result, a rather broad-based cultural problem seems apparent. The work group's culture is holding back performance, satisfaction, and morale in several ways.

COPYRIGHT © 1991–2011 BY ORGANIZATIONAL DESIGN CONSULTANTS. ALL RIGHTS RESERVED.

Continuing with this example, the identified Culture-Gaps suggest the following directions for change and improvement: The technical norms should be changed in the direction of more Task Innovation and more Task Support. Furthermore, it would be helpful to examine behavior in the work group to see if personal needs were taking priority over group goals. If this were evident, a change toward *less* Personal Freedom would be recommended. Specifically, norms could be encouraged that stressed more discipline, more compliance with rules and regulations, and more loyalty to the organization. Such a change might also serve to encourage a movement toward more Task Innovation and more Task Support.

Naturally, making a transition from actual to desired norms cannot be done by simply being aware—intellectually—of what change is needed. Nor will cultural change occur by making public speeches or distributing literature on the subject. Changing a work group's (or department's or organization's) culture takes a systematic and orchestrated effort over an extended period of time. Furthermore, it is difficult—if not impossible—to create lasting cultural change by concentrating only on culture. All the other key features of an organization must be examined and, perhaps, adjusted as well—including skills, teams, strategy-structures, and even the reward system.

See R. H. Kilmann's book, *Quantum Organizations* (Newport Coast, CA: Kilmann Diagnostics, 2011), to learn more about a completely integrated program for systemwide transformation—with managing cultural norms at center stage.

COPYRIGHT © 1991–2011 BY ORGANIZATIONAL DESIGN CONSULTANTS. ALL RIGHTS RESERVED.

Making Culture-Gap® Comparisons

About six months to one year after an effort to change cultural norms has been initiated, it is worthwhile to assess if the identified Culture-Gaps have, in fact, been reduced. Retaking the survey provides a convenient before-and-after comparison for revealing where cultural improvements have occurred and where additional effort is needed.

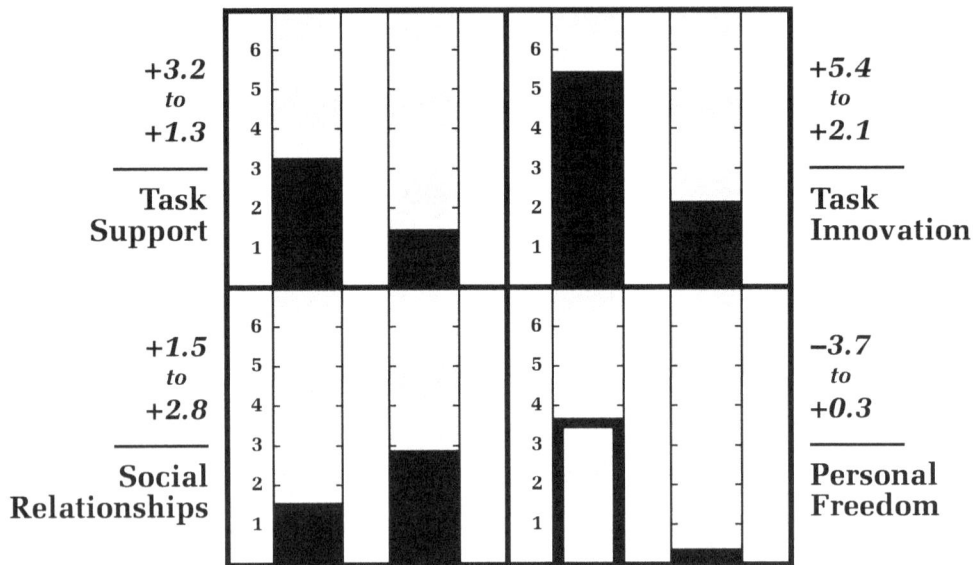

+3.2
to
+1.3
———
Task Support

+1.5
to
+2.8
———
Social Relationships

+5.4
to
+2.1
———
Task Innovation

−3.7
to
+0.3
———
Personal Freedom

Culture-Gap® Comparison

For a systematic process for managing culture-gaps for both the first and second assessment, see: R. H. Kilmann: *Work Sheets for Identifying and Closing Culture-Gaps* (Newport Coast, CA: Kilmann Diagnostics, 2011).

COPYRIGHT © 1991–2011 BY ORGANIZATIONAL DESIGN CONSULTANTS. ALL RIGHTS RESERVED.

Assessment Tools for the Eight Tracks
Distributed by Kilmann Diagnostics

Kilmann-Saxton Culture-Gap® Survey

Kilmanns Organizational Belief Survey

Kilmanns Time-Gap Survey

Kilmanns Team-Gap Survey

Organizational Courage Assessment

Kilmann-Covin Organizational Influence Survey

Plus the Online Version of the
Thomas-Kilmann Conflict Mode Instrument

Plus These Training and Development Tools
Work Sheets for Identifying and Closing Culture-Gaps
Work Sheets for Identifying and Closing Team-Gaps

And the Book That Fully Explains the Eight Tracks
Quantum Organizations

www.ingramcontent.com/pod-product-compliance
Lightning Source LLC
Chambersburg PA
CBHW081205270326
41930CB00014B/3308

* 9 7 8 0 9 8 3 2 7 4 2 1 6 *